A
Dedicated Notebook
for
Daily F-r-e-e-Writing

Weekly/Monthly
F-r-e-e-Writing Reviews

Introduction

F-r-e-e-writing couldn't be simpler. It's writing fast and free about your inner responses to your outer life. It's ideally done by hand, with a pen. Hence, this notebook.

When done regularly, as a dedicated practice, f-r-e-e-writing delivers many proven benefits.

- **F-r-e-e-Writing** = Writing fast, raw, exact and easy.

- **F-r-e-e-Writing Practice** = Writing fast, raw, exact and easy, every day, within a time or page allocation.

Full instructions are given on page iv.

For more, including an in-depth understanding of the practice, its benefits and challenges, exercises and prompts, and answers to frequently asked questions, see the companion book *F-r-e-e-writing: A Creativist Guide*.

The f-r-e-e-writing book and notebook are part of the Go Creative series.
More information:
OrnaRoss.com/my-books/go-creative-series/

F-R-E-E-WRITING INSTRUCTIONS
HOW TO F-R-E-E-WRITE

F-r-e-e-Writing = Writing fast, raw, exact and easy.

F = *Fast*. F-r-e-e-write as fast as you can, without stopping. Keep the pen moving for the allocated time or page count.

R = *Raw*. Don't worry about punctuation, spelling, or keeping within lines. Let whatever wants to be written flow through your pen. Accept it, as it arrives.

E = *Exact*. Go deep into the details. Recall the specific sounds, smells, tastes, thirsts, feelings you experienced. This is your life you're writing about, your way of seeing. Don't hold back.

E = *Easy*. Above all, write freely. Smile, breathe, unclench your jaw, relax your muscles. Let it flow. Let f-r-e-e-writing tell you what you need to know.

F-R-E-E-WRITING PRACTICE
DAILY INSTRUCTIONS

Sit in stillness and quiet, with your notebook open before you, your pen beside it. For two full minutes, sit with silence, letting your breathing become progressively slower and deeper. You are preparing to write f-r-e-e: fast, raw, exact and easy. Let your thoughts settle, enjoying the pause before you begin.

- **Date**: Note the day, month and year

- **Internal Weather**: Turn your attention inward and observe: how are you feeling inside? Use the metaphor of the weather to help you capture your internal state e.g. sunny, clearing after squalls, a little stormy, misting over. All weathers are welcomed, for what they are.

- **F-r-e-e-write for three pages**: You can write about whatever comes to mind (free f-r-e-e-writing). Or you can choose an exercise or writing prompt from the F-r-e-e-writing book or one of the Go Creative guides. Or you can set yourself your own topic.

- **Keep the pen moving**: If you find yourself getting stuck during the session, just keep writing "I can't think what to write, I can't think what to write" and you'll soon find your mind moving again, and your pen following after.

- **Thought For The Day (TFD)**: At the end of each daily session, f-r-e-e-write a quick thought for that day.

F-R-E-E-WRITING PRACTICE
WEEKLY INSTRUCTIONS

- **F-r-e-e-write 18 pages then review**: A f-r-e-e-writing week is six writing days of three pages a day, plus a review. Ideally, you f-r-e-e-write every day so the f-r-e-e-writing week matches the chronological week. Know, however, that you will miss days. Everyone does.

- On the seventh day, review. Full review instructions can be found on the review page.

- **Thought For The Week (TFW)**: At the end of each review, f-r-e-e-write a thought for that week

F-R-E-E-Writing
Week One

Week 1, Day 1

DATE: _____

INTERNAL WEATHER: _____

CTFT:

Week 1, Day 2

Date: _____

Internal Weather: _____

CTFT:

Week 1, Day 3

DATE:

INTERNAL WEATHER:

CTFT:

Week 1, Day 4

DATE: _____

INTERNAL WEATHER: _____

CTFT:

Week 1, Day 5

DATE: _____

INTERNAL WEATHER: _____

CTFT:

Week 1, Day 6

DATE: _____

INTERNAL WEATHER: _____

CTFT:

Review 1 – 1

F-R-E-E-WRITING REVIEW INSTRUCTIONS

A F-r-e-e-writing Review is an active reading back of the previous six day's f-r-e-e-writing, noting insights and intentions. The aim is to observe and note — not to judge. Sharpening your observing mind and softening your judging mind are two key creative skills fostered by f-r-e-e-writing.

- **Read fast:** Read back briskly. Don't get pulled in by what you've written or opinions rising in you about what you've written. This is a chance to absorb the miracles and madnesses of your own mind, with detached amusement.

- **Withhold all judgement**s: Read with a highlighter pen in hand, in a spirit of observation, looking out for ideas, intuitions, insights and intentions to highlight.

- **Note**: Transfer these into the dedicated clouds and waves on the review pages. There is also space for brief notes, sketches or doodles.

- **Appreciate**: Know that no further analysis is necessary. The value in the f-r-e-e-writing review, as in f-r-e-e-writing itself, is simply in the doing.

- **Look back to leap forward**: The thoughts, now expressed in your notebook, have been freed and the new knowledge and insights you've noted will go forward with you into next f-r-e-e-writing notebook.

Imaginings

What if...?

Ideas

What I now think

Insights

What I didn't know I knew

Intentions

What I'm going to do now

F-r-e-e-writing Review

Notes   Sketch

F-R-E-E-Writing
Week Two

Week 2, Day 1

DATE: _____

INTERNAL WEATHER: _____

CTFT:

Week 2, Day 2

DATE: _____

INTERNAL WEATHER: _____

CTFT:

Week 2, Day 3

Date: _____

Internal Weather: _____

CTFT:

Week 2, Day 4

Date: _____

Internal Weather: _____

CTFT:

Week 2, Day 5

DATE: _____

INTERNAL WEATHER: _____

CTFT:

Week 2, Day 6

Date: _____

Internal Weather: _____

CTFT:

Review 2 – 1

F-R-E-E-WRITING REVIEW INSTRUCTIONS

A F-r-e-e-writing Review is an active reading back of the previous six day's f-r-e-e-writing, noting insights and intentions. The aim is to observe and note — not to judge. Sharpening your observing mind and softening your judging mind are two key creative skills fostered by f-r-e-e-writing.

- **Read fast:** Read back briskly. Don't get pulled in by what you've written or opinions rising in you about what you've written. This is a chance to absorb the miracles and madnesses of your own mind, with detached amusement.

- **Withhold all judgement**s: Read with a highlighter pen in hand, in a spirit of observation, looking out for ideas, intuitions, insights and intentions to highlight.

- **Note**: Transfer these into the dedicated clouds and waves on the review pages. There is also space for brief notes, sketches or doodles.

- **Appreciate**: Know that no further analysis is necessary. The value in the f-r-e-e-writing review, as in f-r-e-e-writing itself, is simply in the doing.

- **Look back to leap forward**: The thoughts, now expressed in your notebook, have been freed and the new knowledge and insights you've noted will go forward with you into next f-r-e-e-writing notebook.

Imaginings

What if...?

Ideas

What I now think

Insights

What I didn't know I knew

Intentions

What I'm going to do now

F-r-e-e-writing Review

Notes

Sketch

F-R-E-E-Writing
Week Three

Week 3, Day 1

Date: _____

Internal Weather: _____

CTFT:

Week 3, Day 2

DATE: _____

INTERNAL WEATHER: _____

CTFT:

Week 3, Day 3

DATE:

INTERNAL WEATHER:

CTFT:

Week 3, Day 4

DATE: _____

INTERNAL WEATHER: _____

CTFT:

Week 3, Day 5

DATE: _____

INTERNAL WEATHER: _____

CTFT:

Week 3, Day 6

DATE: _____

INTERNAL WEATHER: _____

CTFT:

Review 3 – 1

F-R-E-E-WRITING REVIEW INSTRUCTIONS

A F-r-e-e-writing Review is an active reading back of the previous six day's f-r-e-e-writing, noting insights and intentions. The aim is to observe and note — not to judge. Sharpening your observing mind and softening your judging mind are two key creative skills fostered by f-r-e-e-writing.

- **Read fast:** Read back briskly. Don't get pulled in by what you've written or opinions rising in you about what you've written. This is a chance to absorb the miracles and madnesses of your own mind, with detached amusement.

- **Withhold all judgement**s: Read with a highlighter pen in hand, in a spirit of observation, looking out for ideas, intuitions, insights and intentions to highlight.

- **Note**: Transfer these into the dedicated clouds and waves on the review pages. There is also space for brief notes, sketches or doodles.

- **Appreciate**: Know that no further analysis is necessary. The value in the f-r-e-e-writing review, as in f-r-e-e-writing itself, is simply in the doing.

- **Look back to leap forward**: The thoughts, now expressed in your notebook, have been freed and the new knowledge and insights you've noted will go forward with you into next f-r-e-e-writing notebook.

Imaginings

What if...?

Ideas

What I now think

Insights

What I didn't know I knew

Intentions

What I'm going to do now

F-r-e-e-writing Review

Notes   Sketch

F-R-E-E-Writing
Week Four

Week 4, Day 1

DATE: _____

INTERNAL WEATHER: _____

CTFT:

Week 4, Day 2

DATE: _____

INTERNAL WEATHER: _____

CTFT:

Week 4, Day 3

DATE: _____

INTERNAL WEATHER: _____

CTFT:

Week 4, Day 4

DATE: _____

INTERNAL WEATHER: _____

CTFT:

Week 4, Day 5

DATE:

INTERNAL WEATHER:

CTFT:

Week 4, Day 6

DATE: _____

INTERNAL WEATHER: _____

CTFT:

Review 4 – 1

F-R-E-E-WRITING REVIEW INSTRUCTIONS

A F-r-e-e-writing Review is an active reading back of the previous six day's f-r-e-e-writing, noting insights and intentions. The aim is to observe and note — not to judge. Sharpening your observing mind and softening your judging mind are two key creative skills fostered by f-r-e-e-writing.

- **Read fast:** Read back briskly. Don't get pulled in by what you've written or opinions rising in you about what you've written. This is a chance to absorb the miracles and madnesses of your own mind, with detached amusement.

- **Withhold all judgement**s: Read with a highlighter pen in hand, in a spirit of observation, looking out for ideas, intuitions, insights and intentions to highlight.

- **Note**: Transfer these into the dedicated clouds and waves on the review pages. There is also space for brief notes, sketches or doodles.

- **Appreciate**: Know that no further analysis is necessary. The value in the f-r-e-e-writing review, as in f-r-e-e-writing itself, is simply in the doing.

- **Look back to leap forward**: The thoughts, now expressed in your notebook, have been freed and the new knowledge and insights you've noted will go forward with you into next f-r-e-e-writing notebook.

Imaginings

What if...?

Ideas

What I now think

Insights

What I didn't know I knew

Intentions

What I'm going to do now

F-r-e-e-writing Review

Notes   Sketch

F-R-E-E-Writing
Week Five

Week 5, Day 1

Date: _____

Internal Weather: _____

CTFT:

Week 5, Day 2

DATE: _____

INTERNAL WEATHER: _____

CTFT:

Week 5, Day 3

DATE: _____

INTERNAL WEATHER: _____

CTFT:

Week 5, Day 4

DATE: _____

INTERNAL WEATHER: _____

CTFT:

Week 5, Day 5

DATE: _____

INTERNAL WEATHER: _____

CTFT:

Week 5, Day 6

DATE: _____

INTERNAL WEATHER: _____

CTFT:

Review 5 – 1

F-R-E-E-WRITING REVIEW INSTRUCTIONS

A F-r-e-e-writing Review is an active reading back of the previous six day's f-r-e-e-writing, noting insights and intentions. The aim is to observe and note — not to judge. Sharpening your observing mind and softening your judging mind are two key creative skills fostered by f-r-e-e-writing.

- **Read fast:** Read back briskly. Don't get pulled in by what you've written or opinions rising in you about what you've written. This is a chance to absorb the miracles and madnesses of your own mind, with detached amusement.

- **Withhold all judgement**s: Read with a highlighter pen in hand, in a spirit of observation, looking out for ideas, intuitions, insights and intentions to highlight.

- **Note**: Transfer these into the dedicated clouds and waves on the review pages. There is also space for brief notes, sketches or doodles.

- **Appreciate**: Know that no further analysis is necessary. The value in the f-r-e-e-writing review, as in f-r-e-e-writing itself, is simply in the doing.

- **Look back to leap forward**: The thoughts, now expressed in your notebook, have been freed and the new knowledge and insights you've noted will go forward with you into next f-r-e-e-writing notebook.

Imaginings

What if...?

Ideas

What I now think

Insights

What I didn't know I knew

Intentions

What I'm going to do now

F-r-e-e-writing Review

Notes   *Sketch*

F-R-E-E-Writing
Week Six

Week 6, Day 1

DATE: _____

INTERNAL WEATHER: _____

CTFT:

Week 6, Day 2

DATE: _____

INTERNAL WEATHER: _____

CTFT:

Week 6, Day 3

DATE:

INTERNAL WEATHER:

CTFT:

Week 6, Day 4

DATE: _____

INTERNAL WEATHER: _____

CTFT:

Week 6, Day 5

DATE: _____

INTERNAL WEATHER: _____

CTFT:

Week 6, Day 6

Date: _____

Internal Weather: _____

CTFT:

Review 6 – 1

F-R-E-E-WRITING REVIEW INSTRUCTIONS

A F-r-e-e-writing Review is an active reading back of the previous six day's f-r-e-e-writing, noting insights and intentions. The aim is to observe and note — not to judge. Sharpening your observing mind and softening your judging mind are two key creative skills fostered by f-r-e-e-writing.

- **Read fast:** Read back briskly. Don't get pulled in by what you've written or opinions rising in you about what you've written. This is a chance to absorb the miracles and madnesses of your own mind, with detached amusement.

- **Withhold all judgement**s: Read with a highlighter pen in hand, in a spirit of observation, looking out for ideas, intuitions, insights and intentions to highlight.

- **Note**: Transfer these into the dedicated clouds and waves on the review pages. There is also space for brief notes, sketches or doodles.

- **Appreciate**: Know that no further analysis is necessary. The value in the f-r-e-e-writing review, as in f-r-e-e-writing itself, is simply in the doing.

- **Look back to leap forward**: The thoughts, now expressed in your notebook, have been freed and the new knowledge and insights you've noted will go forward with you into next f-r-e-e-writing notebook.

Imaginings

What if...?

Ideas

What I now think

Insights

What I didn't know I knew

Intentions

What I'm going to do now

F-r-e-e-writing Review

Notes   Sketch

F-R-E-E-Writing
Week Seven

Week 7, Day 1

Date: _____

Internal Weather: _____

CTFT:

Week 7, Day 2

DATE: _____

INTERNAL WEATHER: _____

CTFT:

Week 7, Day 3

Date: _____

Internal Weather: _____

CTFT:

Week 7, Day 4

Date: _____

Internal Weather: _____

CTFT:

Week 7, Day 5

DATE: _____

INTERNAL WEATHER: _____

CTFT:

Week 7, Day 6

DATE: _____

INTERNAL WEATHER: _____

CTFT:

Review 7 – 1

F-R-E-E-WRITING REVIEW INSTRUCTIONS

A F-r-e-e-writing Review is an active reading back of the previous six day's f-r-e-e-writing, noting insights and intentions. The aim is to observe and note — not to judge. Sharpening your observing mind and softening your judging mind are two key creative skills fostered by f-r-e-e-writing.

- **Read fast:** Read back briskly. Don't get pulled in by what you've written or opinions rising in you about what you've written. This is a chance to absorb the miracles and madnesses of your own mind, with detached amusement.

- **Withhold all judgement**s: Read with a highlighter pen in hand, in a spirit of observation, looking out for ideas, intuitions, insights and intentions to highlight.

- **Note**: Transfer these into the dedicated clouds and waves on the review pages. There is also space for brief notes, sketches or doodles.

- **Appreciate**: Know that no further analysis is necessary. The value in the f-r-e-e-writing review, as in f-r-e-e-writing itself, is simply in the doing.

- **Look back to leap forward**: The thoughts, now expressed in your notebook, have been freed and the new knowledge and insights you've noted will go forward with you into next f-r-e-e-writing notebook.

- You may wish to look back over the other six reviews, to see how things have changed for you over the course of this notebook.

Imaginings

What if...?

Ideas

What I now think

Insights

What I didn't know I knew

Intentions

What I'm going to do now

F-r-e-e-writing Review

Notes

Sketch

ACKNOWLEDGMENTS

A deep bow to everyone who has taken a Go Creative or F-r-e-e-writing Workshop with me. Your writings, discussions and feedback have helped to create this notebook and the book that accompanies it.

Particular thanks to: Lorraine Reid, Helen Langford, Caitlin O'Neill & the SAOL project, Ailbhe Smyth and all at WERRC. And, of course, to the WoW women, especially Kathy Dillon, the WoWest of the WoW, for her love and support and for always getting it -- right from the first moment to the gritty end.

ABOUT THE AUTHOR

Orna Ross is a bestselling and award-winning author and has been named "one of the 100 most influential people in publishing" (The Bookseller), for her work with The Alliance of Independent Authors (ALLi). A long-time facilitator of creative and imaginative practice, she has a dedicated belief in the power of the written word. Born and raised in Ireland, she now lives in London and St Leonard's on Sea.

www.ornaross.com

Books By Orna Ross

NOVELS

After The Rising

Before The Fall

Blue Mercy

Her Secret Rose

POEMS

Poems To Inspire Series

Poems For Christmas (Anthology)

Poems For Mothers (Anthology)

Selected Poetry I

GO CREATIVE SERIES

How To Create Anything

The Psychology of Creative Success

You're Not Crazy, You're Creative...

... and more

GUIDEBOOKS FOR AUTHORS

Successful Self-Publishing Series

Please Give A Short Review

If you've enjoyed, or benefited from f-r-e-e writing, a few words about your experience of the book or this notebook in the form of a review at Amazon or Goodreads would be greatly appreciated.

Author Website: **OrnaRoss.com**

To purchase more f-r-e-e-writing notebooks or books from the Go Creative series: **OrnaRoss.com/my-books/go-creative-series**

To download free Go Creative maps & logs: **OrnaRoss.com/library**

Printed in Great Britain
by Amazon